Modern Sashiko

Silke Bosbach

First published in Great Britain 2015
by Search Press Limited
Wellwood, North Farm Road, Tunbridge Wells,
Kent TN2 3DR

Reprinted 2018

Original German edition published as
Modernes Sashiko

Original edition © 2013 Christophorus Verlag
GmbH & Co. KG, Freiburg

World rights reserved by Christophorus Verlag
GmbH, Freiburg/Germany

English translation by Burravoe Translation Services

ISBN: 978-1-78221-061-0

Designs and projects: Silke Bosbach
Step photos: Atelier Silke Bosbach except p. 7
top: Schoppel/Hohenloher Wolle, p. 12 bottom:
baby lock Deutschland
Model photos and styling: Birgit Völkner
Technical drawings and templates:
Carsten Bachmann

Printed in China through Asia Pacific Offset

Silke Bosbach

Modern Sashiko

Search Press

Dear reader,

Sashiko is a beautiful sewing and embroidery technique that originated in rural Northern Japan many centuries ago. The simple technique consists of basic running stitches and was originally developed for economical purposes to breathe new life into old and repaired fabrics.

Traditionally, sashiko used white running stitches sewn onto dyed indigo fabrics. Today, modern sashiko combines historic designs with contemporary materials (e.g. multicolour threads and felt) and it is no longer necessary for the fabrics to be dyed indigo.

In the first part of this book, an in-depth introduction explains the basic embroidery technique, using decorative models as examples. The second part focuses on modern surface designs on various textile surfaces, combining traditional sashiko with other techniques. The resulting fabrics are very versatile, making beautifully embellished pieces which can either be used for decoration just on their own or as part of larger projects.

You will soon discover how sashiko is, at once, a soothing yet wonderfully practical technique that allows you to create your own blend of the traditional and the modern.

Yours,

Contents

A history of sashiko

A look at the early days of sashiko reveals that only a few original samples of this technique still exist, and those that do are difficult to date and cannot accurately be ascribed to a specific crafter. The reason that so few items still exist is that the textiles were generally used until they wore out completely.

Between 1615 and 1868, sashiko became a popular form of needlework in Japan. The country was finally experiencing some stability after centuries of war and was beginning to enjoy prosperity. It was during this time that sashiko found favour in many rural communities, invigorating old fabrics from bags and work clothing (jackets, waistcoats, socks or gaiters) to everyday items (futon covers, rice bags or cleaning cloths).

Older women instructed young girls and women in sashiko, with endurance and precision considered as important as the actual technique.

In addition to its economic significance, the technique also included a very spiritual dimension. For instance, monks composed prayers for when sashiko was used to sew a *kesa* – a basic undergarment, usually in a dark colour, that is worn by Buddhist monks to this day and consists of several long strips of fabric that are sewn together to make a cloth. Japanese *kesas* serve decorative and symbolic purposes. They differ in appearance depending on the particular school of Buddhism, but also vary according to the occasion and the wearer's rank. The classic shape is a large rectangle with patterns than can be wrapped around the entire body. In everyday life, miniature *kesas* with a tie are often worn like an apron.

Sashiko was also used to embroider the jacket lining of fire fighters' clothing. When a fire had been put out, the jacket was turned inside out and the decorative lining put on display.

Sashiko designs are based on various (symbolic) images: snow-covered ground, Buddhist images, ceramics, textiles (such as pattern books), but also references to architecture. Very many of the traditional sashiko designs symbolise protection against evil spirits, prosperity/wealth or the subject of marriage.

Old sashiko works consist of two or three layers of fabric while modern sashiko usually uses wadding/batting as the lining to create three-dimensional structures.

Around 1950, Japan began to prosper and synthetic fibres became increasingly appealing, while traditional clothing became less well regarded in the country. Sashiko gradually receded into the background, and many textiles were destroyed or disposed of. However, from about 1970, sashiko experienced something of a renaissance, and became a popular choice for quilting.

Today, sashiko is being given an entirely new interpretation in the field of modern textile art.

Materials and tools

You only require a few basic materials and tools in order to produce beautiful sashiko works of art.

You can easily store the following equipment for sewing and marking in a small bag and carry it around with you so that you always have your latest sashiko project with you wherever you go.

Needles and pins

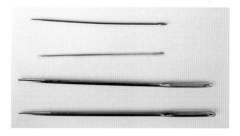

Sharps sewing needles are usually used for sashiko, but you can use **embroidery needles** instead. It is important that the thickness of the fabric, yarn and needles are always matched. Glass-headed pins are also required for marking or pinning together layers of fabric.

Yarns

Sashiko yarn consists of twisted long-staple cotton. A well-stocked retailer will stock sashiko yarn in various thicknesses. High-quality **crochet and knitting yarns** are another excellent option for embroidering modern sashiko.

Thin, dyed **machine embroidery thread** is an excellent alternative to classic crochet and knitting yarns.

Stranded cotton embroidery thread (or floss) is also idea for sashiko embroidery. It is available in lots of colours, and can be used in any number of strands.

Scissors

Modern sashiko ideally uses two types of scissors: one a small pair of **embroidery scissors** that are used to cleanly trim the threads of yarn, and the other a pair of **tailor's scissors** that are used to cut the fabrics. However, a standard pair of craft scissors will suffice for your first attempts at your new hobby.

Materials and tools

Marking pens

A **disappearing marker or craft pen** is ideal for drawing embroidery designs on a light-coloured background, because light and moisture cause the lines to fade. Marking pens with a white tip are more suitable for dark backgrounds (e.g. **chalk pens**). Tailor's chalk can be used on both light and dark fabrics.

Glass or wooden beads

In order to achieve three-dimensional effects, textile bases are backed with **beads** made of wood or glass and then tied in place with thread or wool. This gives the surface a sculpted effect that can be round, oval or rectangular, depending on the beads that you use.

Fabric base

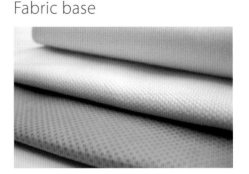

Most fabrics can be used in modern sashiko: you can use either fabrics made of natural fibres of animal, plant or mineral origin, or fibres made from synthetic or chemical fibres. However, the fine texture of cotton and linen fibres makes them ideal for sashiko embroidery.

Felt bases

It is worth making your own thin **felt base**. Try using an unspun wool roving tacked onto a stabilising paper eg. Artfelt® a special kind of paper that dissolves in hot water or you can also use other fibres, such as silk.

Wadding/batting

Wadding/batting is used in modern sashiko projects to create sculptural patterns. A layer of wadding/batting is placed between two pieces of fabric. Traditional sashiko uses several layers of old fabric.

Notes:

Do not use white wadding/batting with dark fabrics. The fleece fibres will penetrate the top layer and make the surface look unattractive.

If making layers of wadding/batting and fabric/felt in combination, it is a good idea to make a sample first to check the ease with which the needle passes through fabrics and fleece. If it does not work the way you want it to, you will either have to use thinner fleece or a different backing fabric.

The sashiko stitch

The sashiko patterns in this book consist of single-stitch sashiko and patterned sashiko, which can be used individually or combined.

Single-stitch sashiko

The designs made with single-stitch sashiko are created as a linear grid with single or multiple strands of yarn. The stitches may cross to create a pattern or have the effect of drifting past each other.

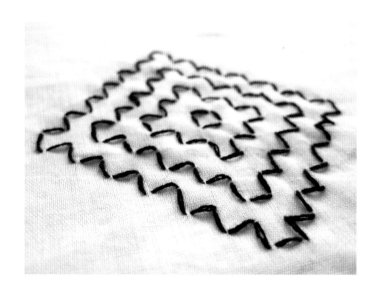

Patterned sashiko

In patterned sashiko, the stitches do not cross. The designs are created from straight or curved lines of running stitch. Patterns are created by changing direction while embroidering. Double or single thread can be used.

Embroidering sashiko

Transferring a design to fabric

There are various ways of transferring a sashiko design to a fabric base. You can draw them free style on the base, or make precise patterns using a ruler and marking pen. With thin and light fabrics, it is a good idea to place the pattern template under the fabric and trace it through. Alternatively, you can transfer your pattern to tissue paper, which can then be layered on your fabric and sewn through, then peeled off afterwards.

If you wish to increase or decrease the size of your sashiko pattern, it is easy to do this on a standard copying machine or printer.

Note:
If you are using any of the patterns in this book, always work from a photocopy. Then you can place the pattern under the fabric and trace over it onto the fabric or attach it to the fabric and sew over the pattern lines.

Tacking fabric layers

If you are using several layers of fabric or wadding/batting, start by tacking the layers of fabric together. Ideally, continue tacking stitches in a star shape all the way to the edge of the fabric.

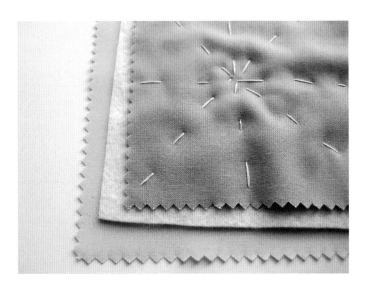

Starting and finishing

Version A – with knots

Tie a knot when starting a row of sashiko, then push the needle through from the back to the front of the fabric and sew. At the end of the sashiko row, draw the needle through to the back of the fabric, wrap the thread once around the needle and draw it tight against the fabric (ideally, holding the needle between your thumb and index finger to form a knot). This will prevent your worked rows from coming undone when pulling the thread. Version A is the safest working method.

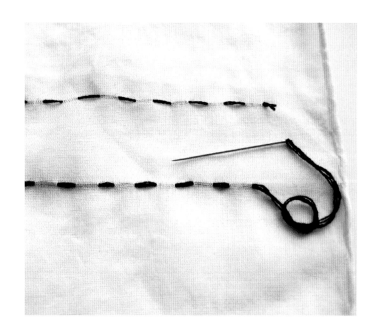

Version B – without knots

Depending on the purpose of your sashiko project, it might be necessary to be able to identify the back and front of it; this is often the case when working with several layers of fabric. In this case, it is better if there are no visible knots in your work.

The method is really simple: to start a row, push the needle through from the back to the front of the fabric a few stitch lengths beyond the point at which you want the sashiko embroidery to begin, leaving a short tail of thread at the back of the work. Stitch back to the starting point, then turn and sew back over these first stitches. Repeat this process in the opposite direction. There will be a double row of stitches at the beginning and end of the line.

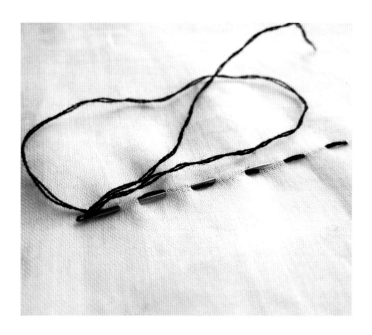

Stitch lengths

In modern sashiko, stitch lengths can vary from small and fine to large and coarse. Often, the stitch length is increased unintentionally in multi-layer works. Between four and eight stitches over a length of 2.5cm (1in) is recommended, worked in a regular structure. With single-stitch sashikos, the stitch length is based on the grid size. In patterned sashiko, the spaces between the stitches should be about half as long as the stitch.

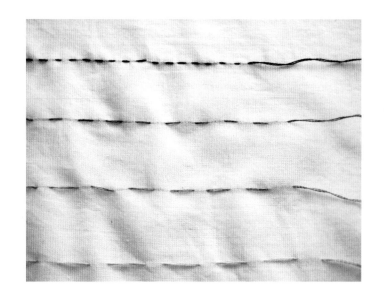

Machine embroidery

A commercial sashiko sewing machine is now available that imitates the human hand. The stitch and space length can be set anywhere between 2 and 5mm ($\frac{1}{16}$ and ¼in), which means that every sewing project will have its own individual character. Using an extenstion table with a wider clearance of 23cm (9in) makes light work even of large quilt or patchwork projects.

The machine uses only a single thread, which is in the bobbin. The sewing needle can be put in a high and low position, and draws the thread through.

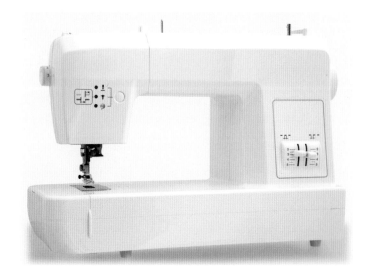

Step by step

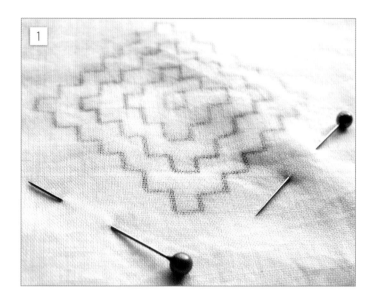

Place the template under the fabric and secure with pins.

Trace the sashiko pattern with a disappearing marker or craft pen.

Start sewing.

The finished sashiko work.

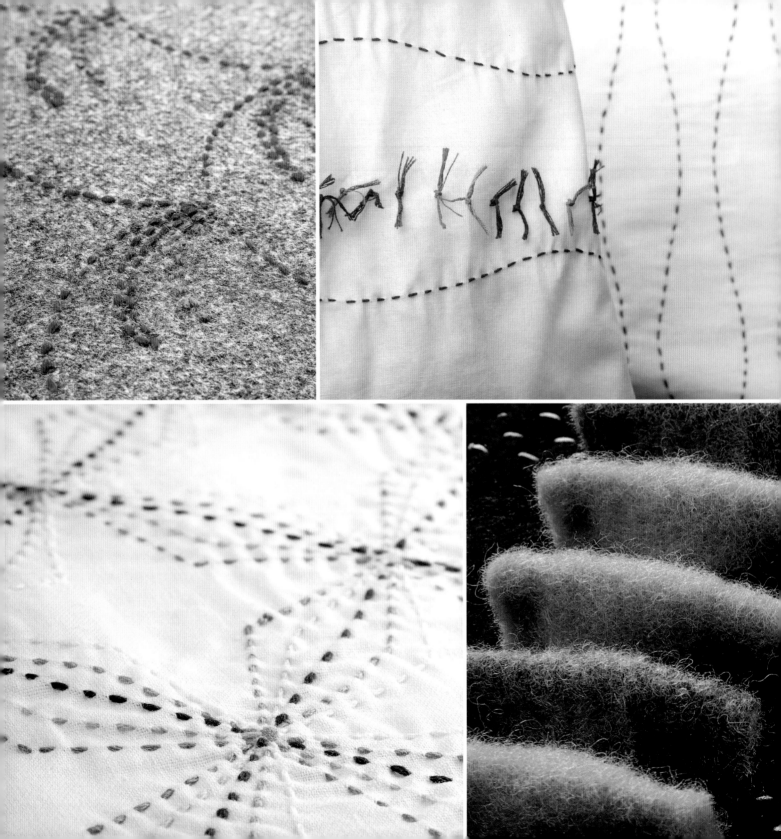

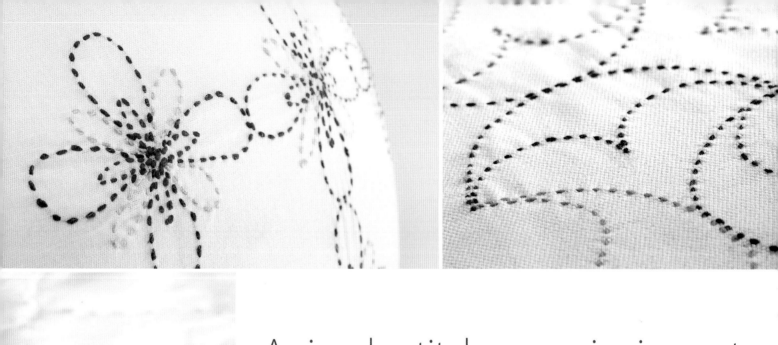

A simple stitch – a major impact

Plain fabrics are magically transformed with simple sashiko stitches, turning bags, pillows and table linen into beautiful works of art.

Floral variations

Small flowery bag · Measurements: 14 x 9.5cm (5½ x 3¾in) · Template no. 1 on page 48

Materials

- Bag made of light cotton, 14 x 9.5cm (5½ x 3¾in)
- Black and beige thread (also light green if desired)
- Basic equipment for marking and sewing (see pages 7 and 8)

How to do it

Transfer the sashiko pattern on to the bag (see page 10), arranging the number and position of flowers as you desire. Try folding the template in half and placing it inside the bag, then you will be able to see the sashiko design quite clearly through the top layer of fabric and trace it through.

Sew the design in tiny sashiko stitches. Black thread adds strong accents, but make sure you do not let it dominate the pattern by using it too much.

Tip:
It is a good idea to use a plain fabric for the bag to show the design at its very best. Fabrics with large patterns can make the floral motifs look lost.

Gentle waves

Pillow in a wavy design · Measurements: 25 x 25cm (9¾ x 9¾in) · Template no. 2 on page 49

Materials

- Light cotton pillow cover, 25 x 25 cm (9¾ x 9¾in)
- Thread in lilac and 7 different berry shades
- Basic equipment for marking and sewing (see pages 7 and 8)
- Matching pillow pad

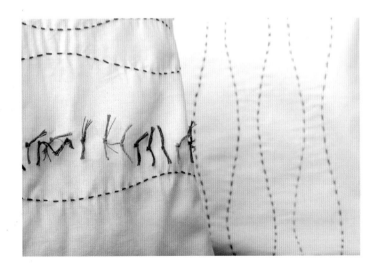

How to do it

Enlarge the template and transfer the sashiko pattern onto the pillow cover (see page 10), choosing the number of wavy lines and the position you desire. Try folding the template to the size of the pillow cover and placing it inside the cover, then you will be able to see the sashiko design quite clearly through the cover and trace the lines. Sew the design in tiny sashiko stitches, using the threads in a set pattern of colours.

When you have finished embroidering, you can work loose threads, either in the centre of the cover and/or along the edges: thread your needle with several strands of embroidery thread, knot the ends, then bring the needle up from the back of the work to the front. Snip the thread, leaving a tail of about 2cm (¾in). Tie the loose threads together in a knot to secure, then trim to the desired length. The loose threads will create a lovely, soft contrast to the boldness of the embroidery. It looks best if you use the same colour pattern with the loose threads as for the sashiko pattern.

Worth knowing:
In Japanese sashiko, the wavy design is called *tatewaku*, which means "cloud of steam".

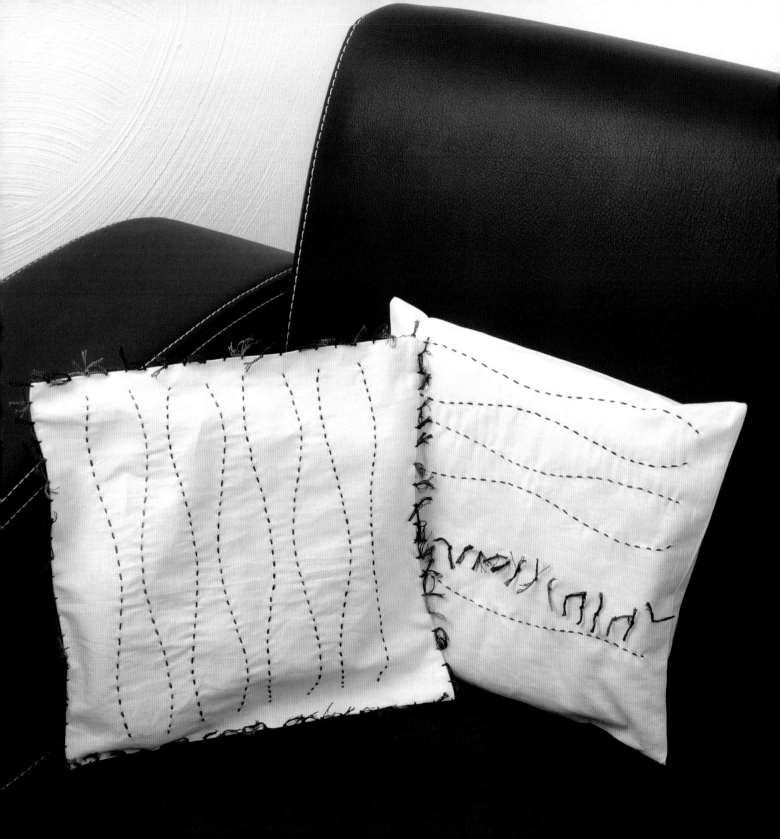

Arc to arc

Batiste scarf with rolling arcs · Measurements: 95 x 95cm (37½ x 37½in) · Template no. 3 on page 50

Materials

- White batiste scarf, 95 x 95cm (37½in x 37½in)
- Gradient sock/3-ply yarn (44% new wool, 14% polyamide, 42% cotton; length 400m/437yds): 100g/3½oz in undyed and green-blue colour range
- Basic equipment for marking and sewing (see pages 7 and 8)

How to do it

Enlarge the template and transfer the sashiko pattern onto the scarf (see page 10). Leave a wide edge unembroidered rather than covering the whole scarf in the pattern.

Sew the design in medium-sized sashiko stitches. First, position the start of the gradient yarn on the needle so that you can sew the pattern and display the full gradient of colour across the surface of the fabric.

Tip:
Plain, simple motifs have a calmer effect than ones that are overloaded with patterns. Remember to take this into account when designing and creating accessories such as scarves and wraps.

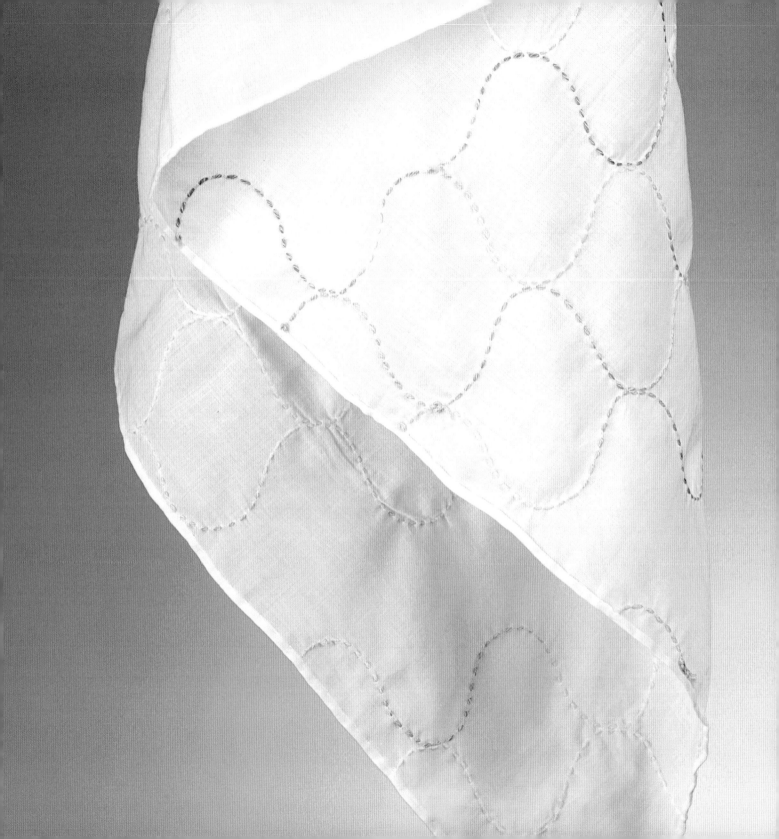

Fishing nets

Place mat in a cross-over design · Measurements: 30 x 40cm (11¾ x 15¾in) · Template no. 4 on page 51

Materials

- Place mat in light fabric, 30 x 40cm (11¾ x 15¾in)
- Gradient lace/1-ply yarn (75% new wool, 25% polyamide, length 800m /875yds): 100g/ 3½oz in black-anthracite-soft grey
- Basic equipment for marking and sewing (see pages 7 and 8)

How to do it

Enlarge the template and transfer the sashiko pattern onto the place mat (see page 10). Choose the number of pattern lines and their postion as desired.

Sew the design in medium-sized sashiko stitches.

Tip:
For a completely different result, sew the sashiko design on the place mat in five to seven strong colours in a rainbow effect.

Flower links

Shopping bag in a floral pattern · Measurements: approximately 28 x 42cm (11 x 16½in) · Template no. 5 on page 52

Materials

- Light cotton bag, approximately 28 x 42 cm (11 x 16½in)
- Thread in pale yellow, orange, bordeaux, pearl green and pearl lilac
- Basic equipment for marking and sewing (see pages 7 and 8)

How to do it

Enlarge the template and transfer the sashiko pattern onto the front of the bag (see page 10). Cover about two-thirds of the area rather than the whole bag, so that the design retains a certain lightness.

Sew the design in medium-sized sashiko stitches, working the pattern lines without changing/breaking the thread. Make sure that a small circle remains open in the middle of the flowers rather than allowing the threads to touch each other.

Grass in the wind

Laptop case with a grass motif · Measurements: 31.5 x 23cm (12½ x 9in) · Template no. 6 on page 53

Materials

- Felt laptop case, approximately 31.5 x 23cm (12½ x 9in) (closed)
- Thread in olive, lilac and raspberry
- Tissue paper
- Basic equipment for marking and sewing (see pages 7 and 8)

How to do it

Enlarge the template and transfer the sashiko pattern to tissue paper. Use pins to secure the pattern piece in the desired position on the felt case.

Embroider the design in medium-sized stitches, making sure that the template does not move; it may be necessary to reattach it with pins from time to time.

In the traditional sequence, the bottom seed head in the design template of an arc motif is sewn first. Then move the thread along the back of the work and sew the top seed head, and finish with the arc. Continue in this way to the end of the row. The seed head can be sewn as a simple line or, as pictured here, in two parallel lines.

On completion of the embroidery, carefully tear the tissue paper away from the felt. If the stitches have been worked evenly, it will be easy to pull the paper off the base.

Tip:
You can also make a laptop case yourself out of felt in just a few steps and at very little cost. Cut out a large piece of felt in the style of an envelope, and attach two press studs to close the bag. You can sew up the sides or use a hot glue gun, leaving a single opening at the top – as with an envelope.

Pear blossom

Ceiling lamp cover with floral design · Measurements: lamp diameter 28cm (11in), fabric cover 35 x 35cm (13¾ x 13¾in)
· Template no. 7 on page 54

Materials

- Firm cotton fabric (e.g. cotton twill) in a light colour, approximately 40 x 40cm (15¾ x 15¾in)
- Threads in brown, rust and sunshine yellow
- Basic equipment for marking and sewing (see pages 7 and 8)
- Half-shell ceiling lamp, approximately 28cm (11in) in diameter
- Hot glue gun
- Iron

How to do it

Enlarge the template and transfer the sashiko pattern onto the fabric (see page 10). Choose the number of motifs and position them as desired.

Using medium-sized sashiko stitches, embroider the outline of the large petals in brown, the medium-sized lines in sunshine yellow and the rest in rust. Make sure that the threads do not touch in the middle of the flowers, but leave a small circle open.

Press the fabric when finished.

Use the hot glue gun to attach the embroidered fabric to the half shell of the ceiling lamp.

Apply the hot glue to the inside (top edge) of the lamp in sections and glue the fabric all around the inside.

Rhythmic rows

Table runner · Measurements: 15 x 40cm (6 x 15¾in)

Materials

- 2-tone felt in black, 3–5mm (²/₁₆–¼in) thick, 15 x 40cm (6 x 15¾in)
- 2-tone felt in light and dark blue, 3–5mm (²/₁₆–¼in) thick, 12 pieces each measuring 3 x 7cm (1¼ x 2¾in)
- White embroidery yarn
- Black and blue sewing thread
- Lined graph paper for the sashiko design template (A4/letter size sheet)
- Basic equipment for marking and sewing (see pages 7 and 8)

How to do it

Using blue thread, sew the blue felt strips into small tubes. Use black sewing thread to sew these tubes to the middle of the black side of the large felt strip at regular intervals.

Cut out a square or rectangle of lined graph paper in the desired size; this will be your template when embroidering the vertical pattern rows.

Pin the lined graph paper to the black felt strip. Using white embroidery yarn, sew vertical rows along the grid lines. The positions of the stitches and spaces of every second row are offset from those in the first row.

Work as many patterned areas as desired.

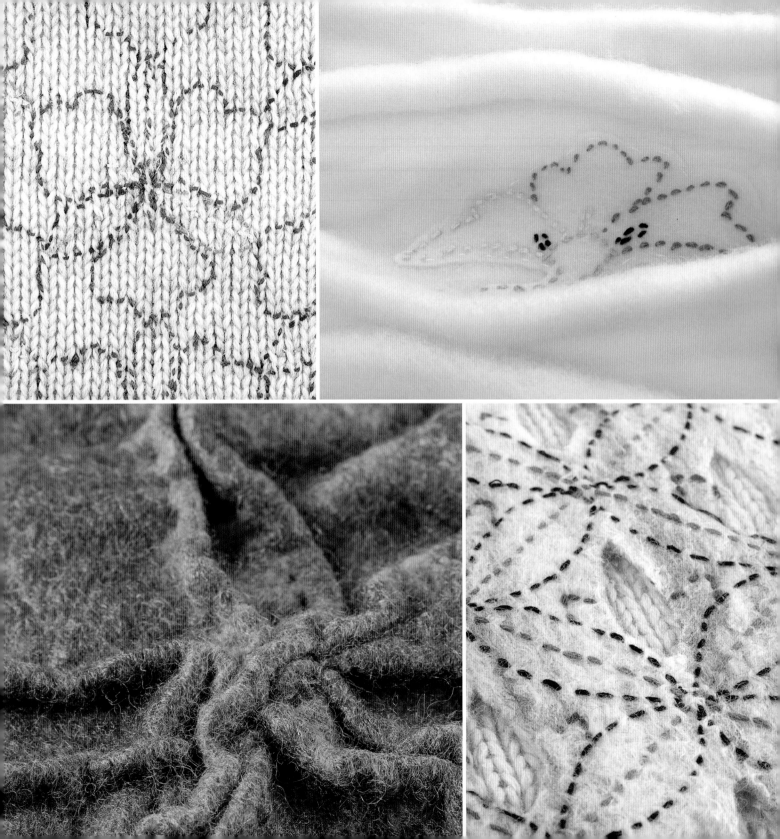

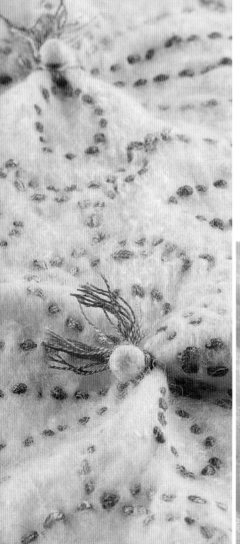

Artistic surface designs

In this section you will be shown how to do sashiko on various textured fabrics, such as felt, knitted fabrics and fleece, and how to use it in combination with other techniques to create fascinating surfaces.

Shining suns

Sashiko and shibori on felt · Template no. 8 on page 55

Materials

- Felt base made of cashmere felt (35% cashmere, 45% merino wool, 20% silk): 50g (1¾oz) in a beige marl
- Wool yarn in sunshine yellow and peach
- Basic equipment for marking and sewing (see pages 7 and 8)
- 8–10 glass beads, approximately 3mm (²/₁₆in) diameter

How to do it

Enlarge the template and transfer the sashiko pattern onto the felt.

Sew over the sashiko motif (with peach yarn for the petals on the inside and sunshine yellow yarn for the outside petals). Do not sew over the inner design ring – make sure to leave it clear.

Position a glass bead under the fabric in the middle of each flower motif holding it tightly in place and, following the diagram below, use wool yarn in both yellow and peach thread to tie the felt around the beads.

Trim the ends of the wool yarn to approximately 1cm (½in) in length and fringe the ends as shown.

Worth knowing:

The tying method used for this item originate from the traditional Japanese *shibori* technique, an ancient tying and dyeing technique in which textiles were tied around plant seeds, which left areas clear.

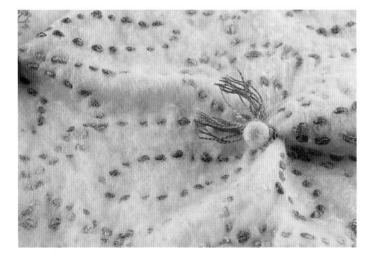

Three-dimensional

Sashiko on decorative organza · Template no. 9 on page 56

Materials

- Decorative organza in beige, olive and copper, each approximately 90 x 100cm (35½ x 39½in)
- Light green and purple thread
- Basic equipment for marking and sewing (see pages 7 and 8)
- Metallic thread in copper
- 1 round wooden bead, approximately 5mm (¼in) in diameter

How to do it

Layer the organza with the copper at the bottom, then the olive and the beige on top. Place a wooden bead beneath the layers of organza.

Pinch the organza layers around the wooden beed, pushing it into the fabric. Hold the bead tightly in place and tie the organza layers around the bead with a length of metallic thread (see Figure 1).

Starting from the top of the bead, cut the fabric layers down to approximately 5mm (¼in) from the tie, dissecting the sphere into four equal-sized sections (see Figure 2).

Push the wooden bead out of the cut area. Fold out the individual layers of fabric to create a lovely flower shape. Repeat the cutting and tying with your wooden bead as often as desired.

Enlarge the template and place it under the organza. Draw the individual sashiko flower patterns among the 3D flowers, and sew using tiny sashiko stitches using purple thread for the larger flowers and light green for the remaining lines.

Figure 1

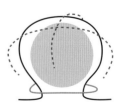

Figure 2

Floral relief

Sashiko pleats on felt · Template no. 10 on page 57

Materials

- Felt base (e.g. from a wool/linen blend) in undyed cotton or berry, approximately 45 x 70cm (17¾ x 27½in)
- Sewing thread to match the felt
- Tissue paper
- Basic equipment for sewing and making (see pages 7 and 8)

How to do it

Enlarge the template and transfer the sashiko pattern to tissue paper. Attach it to the felt base, securing it with pins.

Pinch the felt to align with the pattern template, making folds approximately 5mm (¼in) deep.

Sew the folds in thread to match the fabric using small, regular sashiko stitches.

Fold individual circles in pleats around the flowers and again sew them in small sashiko stitches.

Carefully tear the tissue paper away from the felt.

Note:
In keeping with the understated style, there should be no more than three flowers per felt base.

Bamboo

Sashiko on knitwear and felt · Template no. 11 on page 58

Materials

- Felt base (eg. from merino wool and silk blend) in grey marl, approximately 35 x 80cm (13¾ x 31½in)
- Tissue paper
- Embroidery thread in peach, black and dark green
- Knitted cashmere scarf (hand or machine knitted) in pale pink, approximately 30 x 75cm (11¾ x 29½in)
- Basic equipment for marking and sewing (see pages 7 and 8)
- Thin sewing thread in soft grey
- Nail scissors

How to do it

Place the felt on top of the scarf and join the two together around the edges, using delicate stitches.

Enlarge the template and transfer it onto tissue paper, then pin it onto the felt base.

Sew the straight lines in fine sashiko stitches on the felt surface using the peach thread. Work the outer semi-circular lines in black thread. Then sew the 'v' shapes in dark green thread.

Use the nail scissors to cut the unembroidered bamboo leaf from the felt layer on every sashiko shape, taking care not to cut into the knitted fabric or the embroidery below it.

When you have finished, carefully remove the tissue paper from the embroidered base.

Wisteria

Sashiko on knit • Template no. 12 on page 59

Materials

- Knitted base (e.g. a knitted scarf in new wool), natural marl
- Tissue paper
- Knitting wool in rosewood, pale pink, chestnut and 4 different shades of blue
- Basic equipment for marking and sewing (see pages 7 and 8)
- Pins

How to do it

Enlarge the template and transfer the sashiko pattern onto tissue paper. Place the tissue paper on the knitted base and secure it with pins.

Sew along the three lines in the middle of every flower in pale pink, rosewood and chestnut using medium-sized sashiko stitches. Be sure not to sew through the centre of the flower pattern.

Sew the large petals and three small leaves in the four shades of blue, again using medium-sized sashiko stitches.

When you have finished sewing, carefully tear the paper away from the knitted base, making sure you do not accidentally pull up any of the stitches.

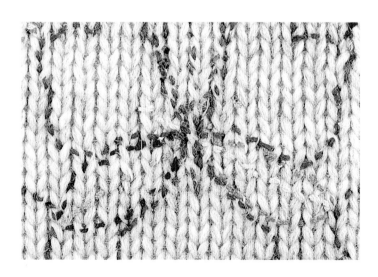

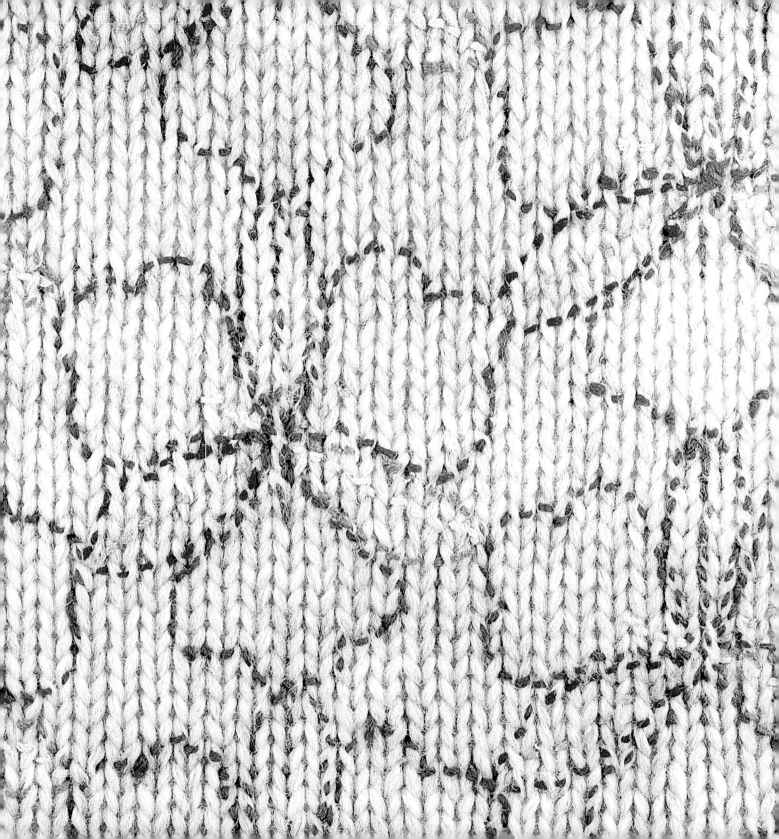

Six-pointed stars

White-on-white sashiko (machine sewn) · Template no. 13 on page 60

Materials

- Crafting felt in white (A4/letter size format)
- Tissue paper
- Firm wadding/batting in white, medium strength (A4/letter size format)
- White sewing thread
- Sashiko sewing machine
- Pins

How to do it

Enlarge the template and transfer the sashiko pattern onto tissue paper (see page 10). Layer the fabric in a textile 'sandwich' as follows: paper template (design face down), crafting felt (for stabilisation), wadding/batting (will become the surface of the design later on). Secure everything with pins.

Turn the layers over and sew the pattern in white thread on the sewing machine.

On completion, carefully tear the tissue paper away from the embroidery. The wadding/batting now forms the surface of the work and you can add further decoration to it if you wish.

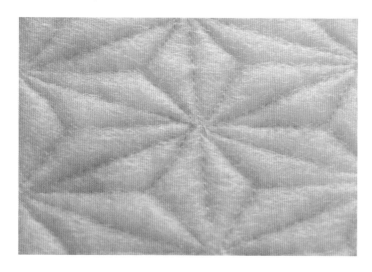

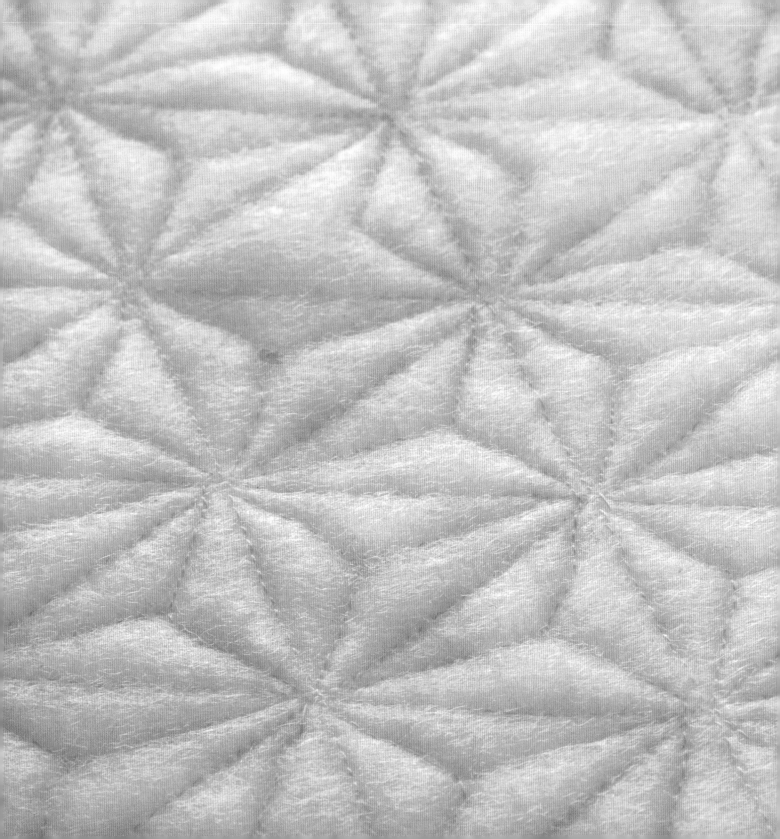

Crane flowers

Sashiko and tucking · Template no. 14 on page 61

Materials

- Crafting felt, undyed, approximately 30 x 40cm (11¾ x 15¾in)
- Firm needle-felted undyed fleece, approximately 60 x 80cm (23½ x 31½in)
- Embroidery thread in sand, yellow, pale pink, pea green and bordeaux
- Basic equipment for marking and sewing (see pages 7 and 8)
- Pins

How to do it

Enlarge the template and transfer as many single flowers on to the crafting felt as you like (see page 10).

Sew the design in small sashiko stitches choosing the colours for the individual areas randomly and avoiding using a specific colour pattern for each design.

When you have completed the floral motifs, cut out the embroidered flowers leaving approximately 3–4mm (⅛ – ³⁄₁₆ in) all around.

Sew the needle-felted fleece in tucks of about 1–2cm (½ – ¾in), leaving enough space between them for the cut-out flowers. In order to achieve a diamond shape, tack two opposing tucks together with a simple stitch at regular intervals.

Sew the cut-out sashiko flowers into the diamond shapes, using the traditional sashiko stitch.

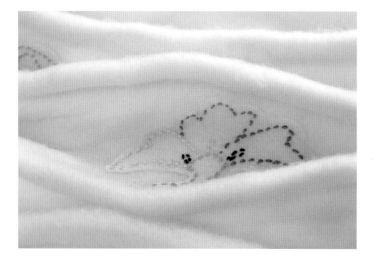

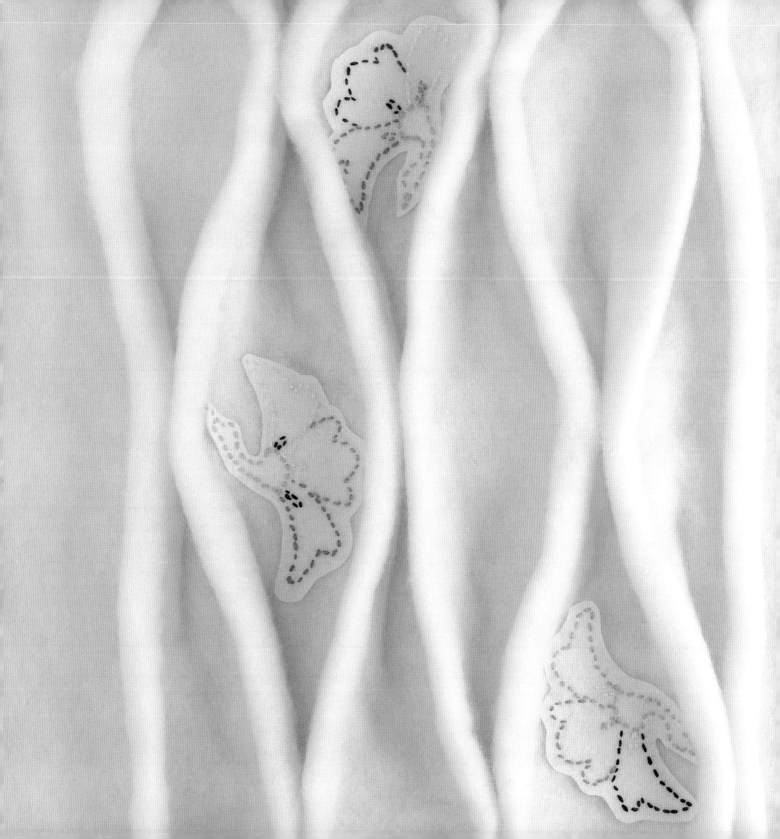

Templates

1

Page 16

2

Page 18

Enlarge template to 200%

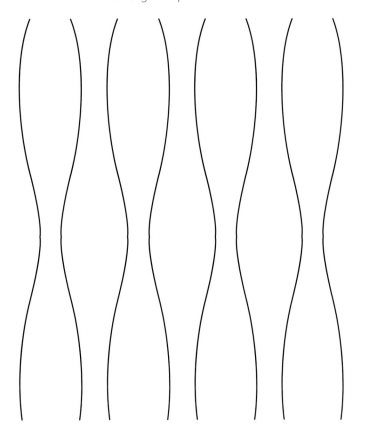

3

Page 20

Enlarge template to 200%

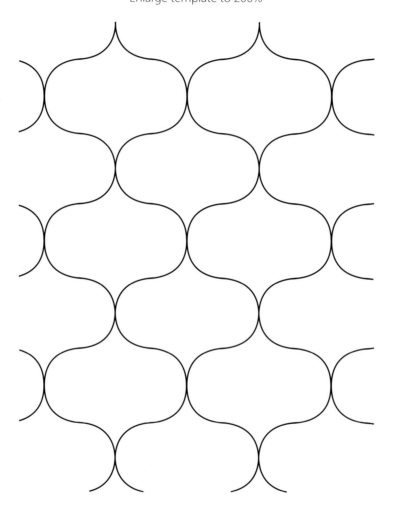

4

Page 22
Enlarge template to 200%

5

Page 24

Enlarge template to 200%

6

Page 26
Enlarge template to 200%

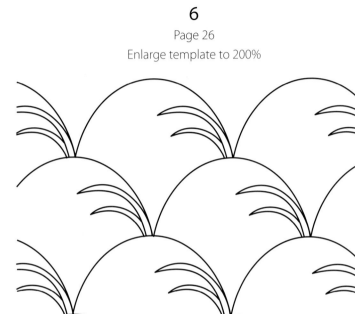

7

Page 28
Enlarge template to 200%

8

Page 34

Enlarge template to 200%

11

Page 40

Enlarge template to 200%

12

Page 42

Enlarge template to 200%

14

Page 46
Enlarge template to 200%